S0-BLQ-577

Famous Black Quotations®

on women, love and other topics

selected and compiled

by

JANET CHEATHAM BELL

SABAYT PUBLICATIONS

Chicago, Illinois

Grateful acknowledgment is made to those who granted permission to reprint substantial excerpts from published works; and to people of African descent throughout the world and through the ages who eloquently express themselves orally and in print.

See acknowledgments on page 99.

Printed and bound in the United States of America.

First edition 9 8 7 6 5 4 3 2 1

ISBN: 0-9616649-3-2

Library of Congress Catalog Card Number: 91-61334

Sabayt Publications, Inc.
P.O. Box 64898
Chicago, Illinois 60664-0898

In memory of my parents
   Smith Henry and Annie Halyard
   CHEATHAM
who passed on to me all that they knew
from their ancestors, plus what they
learned on their own.

Comparisons of human genes worldwide have
produced a "family tree" of the human race
whose branches closely mirror the branching of
languages proposed by linguists, leading to the
startling suggestion that all people—and
perhaps all languages—are descended from a
tiny population that lived in Africa some
200,000 years ago.

William F. Allman
U.S. News & World Report
November 5, 1990

CONTENTS

PREFACE

When I published *Famous Black Quotations; and some not so famous* in 1986, I hoped that it would be welcomed as a convenient source of quotations by people of African descent and that enough of them would be sold to pay for production costs. To my surprise and deep satisfaction, that book has been received enthusiastically, and is currently in its fourth printing and selling well. We have received hundreds of encouraging letters in response to the publication. Gwendolyn Brooks, Poet Laureate of Illinois; former U.S. Representative Shirley Chisholm; the late

Dr. St. Clair Drake, Stanford University Professor Emeritus; Earl G. Graves, publisher of *Black Enterprise*; and Susan L. Taylor, Editor-in-Chief of *Essence*, were among the many who wrote.

For those of you who were disappointed that there were no quotations about love in the first book, this collection is especially for you. When the manuscript for the first book became too long, the quotations on Women and Love were set aside for another book.

This compilation of over 200 new quotations arranged in six different categories represents primarily what caught my eyes and ears as I read and listened. Several of the quotations include the year in which they first appeared. That information is used when the date provides additional illumination for the quotation. Obviously, a collection of this size makes no claim to being either exhaustive or comprehensive, yet I have attempted to offer a range of thought, limited, of course, by my own human inability to read everything and be everywhere.

Several people brought me quotations, many of which are included here. In that regard, I especially want to thank Judith Ball, Arlene Williams, Ron Watkins, and my son, W. Kamau Bell. I must also express my gratitude to Alvin Foster, Madeline Scales-Taylor, Delores Logan Watson, Edna Pruce, Lee McCord, my brother James, Arlene and Kamau, whose encouragement and assistance have been essential to my perserverance; and to Ursula McPike, who kindly reads everything and gives me necessary feedback. Thanks as well to Reggie, Rosie and Walter, who consistently provide opportunities for me to grow.

J.C.B.

WOMEN

Next to God we are
indebted to women, first
for life itself, and then for
making it worth living.

MARY MCLEOD BETHUNE

I'm a woman
Phenomenally
Phenomenal woman
That's me

MAYA ANGELOU

The present mincing horror at free
womanhood must pass if we are
ever to be rid of the bestiality of free
manhood. . . .

W.E.B. DUBOIS, *1920*

The race cannot succeed, nor build
strong citizens, until we have a race
of women competent to do more
than bear a brood of negative men.

T. THOMAS FORTUNE

We are free to say that in respect to political rights, we hold women to be justly entitled to all we claim for men.

FREDERICK DOUGLASS, *1848*

Living in a society where the objective social position and the reputed virtues of white women smother whatever worth black women may have, the Negro male is put to judging his women by what he sees and imagines the white woman is.

CALVIN HERNTON, *1965*

To the ordinary American or Englishman, the race question at bottom is simply a matter of ownership of women; white men want the right to use all women, colored and white, and they resent the intrusion of colored men in this domain.

W.E.B. DUBOIS

When you're a black woman, you seldom get to do what you just want to do; you always do what you have to do.

DOROTHY I. HEIGHT

That man over there says that women need to be helped into carriages, and lifted over ditches, and to have the best place everywhere. Nobody ever helps me into carriages, or over mud-puddles, or gives me any best place! And ain't I a woman?

SOJOURNER TRUTH, *1851*

I do not see how colored women can be true to themselves unless they demand recognition for themselves and those they represent.

IDA B. WELLS-BARNETT

Women manage, quite brilliantly, on the whole, and to stunning and unforeseeable effect, to survive and surmount being defined by others. They dismiss the definition, however dangerous or wounding it may be—or even, sometimes, find a way to utilize it—perhaps because they are not dreaming. But men are neither so supple nor so subtle. A man fights for his manhood: that's the bottom line.

JAMES BALDWIN

Only the black woman can say, "When and where I enter, . . . then and there the whole race enters with me."

ANNA JULIA COOPER, *1892*

There is a great stir about colored men getting their rights but not a word about colored women; and if colored men get their rights and not colored women theirs, you see, colored men will be masters over the women.

SOJOURNER TRUTH

Black women are not here to compete or fight with you, brothers. If we have hangups about being male or female, we're not going to be able to use our talents to liberate all of our black people.

SHIRLEY CHISHOLM

For as unseemly as it may appear now-a-days for a woman to preach, it should be remembered that nothing is impossible with God.

JARENA LEE, *1836*

The future woman must have a life work and economic independence. She must have knowledge. She must have the right of motherhood at her own discretion.

W.E.B. DUBOIS, *1920*

Throughout the social history of black women, children are more important than marriage in determining the woman's domestic role.

PAULA GIDDINGS

I had . . . found that motherhood was a profession by itself, just like schoolteaching and lecturing. . . .

IDA B. WELLS-BARNETT

Momma . . . rose alone
to apocalyptic silence,
set the sun in our windows
and daily mended the world. . . .

PAULETTE CHILDRESS WHITE

You go through so many changes
as a child, then you grow up and
discover that none of that stuff
mattered, except for the impression
it made on your mind.

JOAN WALTON COLLASO

In search of my mother's garden, I
found my own.

ALICE WALKER

When in this world a man comes
forward with a thought, a deed, a
vision, we ask not how does he look,
but what is his message? . . . The
world still wants to ask that a
woman primarily be pretty. . . .

W.E.B. DUBOIS, *1920*

When you grab hold to a woman,
you got something there. You got a
whole world there. You got a way of
life kicking up under your hand.
That woman take and make you feel
like something.

AUGUST WILSON

And God said: Adam,
What hast thou done? . . .
and Adam
With his head hung down,
Blamed it on the woman.

JAMES WELDON JOHNSON

All womanhood is hampered today because the world on which it is emerging is a world that tries to worship both virgins and mothers and in the end despises motherhood and despoils virgins.

W.E.B. DUBOIS, *1920*

When we will, women won't; and when we won't, they want to exceedingly.

TERENCE *(Publius Terentius Afer)*

Small nations are like indecently dressed women. They tempt the evil-minded.

JULIUS NYERERE

Sisters have taught me that we should listen to the poetry within, capture and express our inner beauty as part of our political and social being.

MANNING MARABLE

But what of black women? . . . I most sincerely doubt if any other race of women could have brought its fineness up through so devilish a fire.

W.E.B. DUBOIS

Perhaps she was both child and
woman, darkness and light, past
and present, life and death—all the
opposites contained and reconciled
in her.

PAULE MARSHALL

I am a black woman
the music of my song
some sweet arpeggio of tears
is written in a minor key
and I
can be heard humming in the night
Can be heard
            humming
in the night

MARI EVANS

LOVE

I leave you love. Love builds. It is positive and helpful. It is more beneficial than hate. Injuries quickly forgotten quickly pass away. Personally and racially, our enemies must be forgiven. . . .

MARY MCLEOD BETHUNE

Along with the idea of romantic love, she was introduced to another—physical beauty. Probably the most destructive ideas in the history of human thought. Both originated in envy, thrived in insecurity, and ended in disillusion. In equating physical beauty with virtue, she stripped her mind, bound it, and collected self-contempt by the heap. She forgot lust and simple caring for. She regarded love as possessive mating, and romance as the goal of the spirit. It would be for her a wellspring from which she would draw the most destructive emotions, deceiving the lover and seeking to imprison the beloved, curtailing freedom in every way.

TONI MORRISON

To love is to make of one's heart a swinging door.

HOWARD THURMAN

I have a strong suspicion . . . that much that passes for constant love is a golded-up moment walking in its sleep.

ZORA NEALE HURSTON

Romance
without finance
don't stand a chance.

AFRICAN-AMERICAN FOLK SAYING

Being black [is] not enough. It [takes] more than a community of skin color to make your love come down on you.

ZORA NEALE HURSTON

Is it true the ribs can tell
The kick of a beast from a
Lover's fist?

MAYA ANGELOU

Love is or it ain't. Thin love ain't love at all.

TONI MORRISON

Nothing that God ever made is the same thing to more than one person. That is natural. There is no single face in nature, because every eye that looks upon it, sees it from its own angle. So every man's spice-box seasons his own food.

ZORA NEALE HURSTON

Love always sees more than is in evidence at any moment of viewing.

HOWARD THURMAN

Love supersedes all armies.

DICK GREGORY

. . . Love is a rock against the wind
Not soft like silk and lace.

ETHERIDGE KNIGHT

I refuse to accept the view that
mankind is so tragically bound to
the starless midnight of racism and
war that the bright daybreak of
peace and brotherhood can never
become a reality . . . I believe that
unarmed truth and unconditional
love will have the final word.

MARTIN LUTHER KING, JR.

War is not the answer, for only love
can conquer hate.

MARVIN GAYE

Violence as a way of achieving racial justice is both impractical and immoral. It is impractical because it is a descending spiral ending in destruction for all. . . . It is immoral because it seeks to humiliate the opponent rather than win his understanding; it seeks to annihilate rather than to convert. Violence is immoral because it thrives on hatred rather than love. . . .

MARTIN LUTHER KING, JR.

Remember, to hate, to be violent, is demeaning. It means you're afraid of the other side of the coin—to love and be loved.

JAMES BALDWIN

Not to fight at all is to choose a weapon by which one fights. Perhaps the authentic moral stature of a man is determined by his choice of weapons which he uses in his fight against the adversary. Of all weapons, love is the most deadly and devastating, and few there be who dare trust their fate in its hands.

HOWARD THURMAN

All you need in the world is love and laughter. That's all anybody needs. To have love in one hand and laughter in the other.

AUGUST WILSON

We must turn to each other and not on each other.

JESSE L. JACKSON

If you can't hold [children] in your arms, please hold them in your heart.

CLARA MCBRIDE HALE

What did I know, what did I know of love's austere and lonely offices?

ROBERT HAYDEN

The guilty furtive European notion
of sex . . . obliterates any possibility
of communion, or any hope of love.

JAMES BALDWIN

Nothing is so much to be shunned
as sex relations.

SAINT AUGUSTINE

We have attempted to separate the
spiritual and the erotic, thereby
reducing the spiritual to a world of
flattened affect, a world of the
ascetic who aspires to feel nothing.

AUDRE LORDE

True rebels, after all, are as rare as
true lovers, and, in both cases, to
mistake a fever for a passion can
destroy one's life.

JAMES BALDWIN

Never offer your heart
to someone who eats hearts. . . .

sail away to Africa
where holy women
await you
on the shore—
long having practiced the art
of replacing hearts
with God
and Song.

ALICE WALKER

One who has no sense of being an object of love is seriously handicapped in making someone else an object of his love.

HOWARD THURMAN

Descendant of slave and of slave owner, I had already been called poet, lawyer, teacher, and friend. Now I was empowered to minister the sacrament of One in whom there is no north or south, no black or white, no male or female—only the spirit of love and reconciliation drawing us all toward the goal of human wholeness.

PAULI MURRAY

Men

I have always thanked God
for making me a man, but
Martin Delany always
thanked God for making
him a black man.

FREDERICK DOUGLASS

Men are not women, and a man's balance depends on the weight he carries between his legs.

JAMES BALDWIN

No white person knows, really knows, how it is to grow up as a Negro boy in the South. The taboo of the white woman eats into the psyche, erodes away significant portions of boyhood sexual development, alters the total concept of masculinity, and creates in the Negro male a hidden ambivalence towards all women, black as well as white.

CALVIN HERNTON, *1965*

I found that what the white man of the South practiced as all right for himself, he assumed to be unthinkable in white women.

IDA B. WELLS-BARNETT, *1927*

It began to seem, indeed, not entirely frivolously, that the only thing which prevented the South from being an absolutely homosexual community was, precisely, the reverberating absence of men.

JAMES BALDWIN

That little man says women can't have as much rights as men, 'cause Christ wasn't a woman! Where did your Christ come from? Where did your Christ come from? From God and a woman! Man had nothing to do with Him.

SOJOURNER TRUTH, *1851*

A man without force is without the essential dignity of humanity. Human nature is so constituted, that it cannot honor a helpless man, though it can pity him, and even this it cannot do long if signs of power do not arise.

FREDERICK DOUGLASS, *1892*

In those days men left their women
for all sorts of reasons . . . and
nobody blamed them much,
because times were hard.

RITA DOVE

The harder you try to hold onto
them, the easier it is for some gal
to pull them away.

AUGUST WILSON

That marvelously mocking, salty
authority with which black men
walked was dictated by the tacit and
shared realization of the price each
had paid to be able to walk at all.

JAMES BALDWIN

I am convinced that the black man will only reach his full potential when he learns to draw upon the strengths and insights of the black woman.

MANNING MARABLE

She's just using him to keep from being by herself. That's the worst use of a man you can have.

AUGUST WILSON

His care suggested a family relationship rather than a man's laying claim.

TONI MORRISON

If you are wise and seek to make your house stable, love your wife fully and righteously. . . . Kindness and consideration will influence her better than force.

THE HUSIA

Bad judgment and carelessness are not punishable by rape.

PEARL CLEAGE

Mothers raise their daughters and let their sons grow up.

AFRICAN-AMERICAN FOLK SAYING

Only men can develop boys into men.

JAWANZA KUNJUFU

A man ain't nothing but a man, but a son? Well now, that's *somebody*.

TONI MORRISON

Fathers and sons arrive at that relationship only by claiming that relationship: that is by paying for it. If the relationship of father to son could really be reduced to biology, the whole earth would blaze with the glory of fathers and sons.

JAMES BALDWIN

but you were the son of a needy father,
the father of a needy son,
you gave her all you had
which was nothing. . . .

LUCILLE CLIFTON

A man must defend himself, if only
to demonstrate his fitness to defend
anything else.

FREDERICK DOUGLASS

The male cannot bear very much
humiliation; and he really cannot
bear it, it obliterates him.

JAMES BALDWIN

Sooner or later all men bark.

OCTAVIA SAINT LAURENT

If men could become pregnant, abortion would be a sacrament.

FLO KENNEDY

When a man keeps beating me to the draw mentally, he begins to get glamorous.

ZORA NEALE HURSTON

What the [small boy] needs to know is that there are men in this world who are like him, black men, African-American men, who read and write and find the whole process of academics something valuable. . . . The epidemic of academic failure in the African-American male population is not going to stop unless we, African-American men, begin to do the job that we can do.

SPENCER HOLLAND

Young single black men can either represent a positive progressive force or one that just continues to react to crisis after crisis.

HAKI R. MADHUBUTI

Black men must simultaneously shoulder some of the blame for their predicament and some of the responsibility for developing personal intervention strategies that will better their condition. . . . As black males, we have become partners in our demise.

THOMAS A. PARHAM

It is perhaps one of the great ironies of my life that so much of it has been spent trying on the one hand to get people to see me as a black man, and on the other not to write me off or apply some damnable double standard when they do.

SYLVESTER MONROE

Studies that bring clarity and
direction to the black male situation
as an integral part of the black
family/community are unpopular,
not easy to get published and very
dangerous.

HAKI R. MADHUBUTI

One thing they cannot prohibit—
The strong men . . . coming on
The strong men gittin' stronger.
Strong men. . . .
Stronger. . . .

STERLING BROWN, *1932*

LIVING IN AMERICA

The bright joyous dreams of
freedom to the slave faded—
were sadly altered, in the
presence of that stern,
practical mother, reality.

ELIZABETH KECKLEY, *1868*

I do not believe that the meaning of the Constitution was forever "fixed" at the Philadelphia Convention. . . . To the contrary, the government they devised was defective from the start, requiring several amendments, a civil war and momentous social transformation to attain the system of constitutional government, and its respect for the individual freedoms and human rights we hold as fundamental today.

THURGOOD MARSHALL

America doesn't respect anything but money. . . . What our people need is a few millionaires.

MADAME C.J. WALKER

The Supreme Court has surrendered. . . . It has destroyed the Civil Rights Bill, and converted the Republican party into a party of money rather than a party of morals.

FREDERICK DOUGLASS, *1894*

Democracy, like religion, never was designed to make . . . profits less.

ZORA NEALE HURSTON

Learning to take hold of one's life is very difficult in a culture that values property over life.

HAKI R. MADHUBUTI

Those forces which stand against the freedom of nations are not only wrong—they are doomed to utter defeat and dishonor. . . . Colored peoples of the world are going to be free and equal no matter whose "best interests" are in the way.

PAUL ROBESON, *1958*

The study of economic oppression led me to realize that Negroes were not alone but were part of an unending struggle for human dignity the world over.

PAULI MURRAY

For as long as whites enforce equality in the price of railroad tickets, and in every other particular, where we are required to pay and do, and be punished, some of us will believe that equality should be carried to a finish.

HENRY MCNEAL TURNER, *1895*

I believe in gradualism, but 90-odd years is gradual enough.

THURGOOD MARSHALL, *1956*

Madison Avenue is afraid of the dark.

NAT "KING" COLE, *1957*

In the South they don't care how close you get, as long as you don't get too high. In the North, they don't care how high you get, as long as you don't get too close.

AFRICAN-AMERICAN FOLK SAYING

When you are fighting for justice and democracy; color, race, and social class have little importance. . . . Man taken in his totality transcends questions of race.

JEAN-BERTRAND ARISTIDE

We would not underestimate the achievements of the captains of industry who . . . have produced the wealth necessary to ease and comfort; but we would give credit to the Negro who so largely supplied the demand for labor by which these things have been accomplished.

CARTER G. WOODSON

How unjust it is, that they who have but little should be always adding something to the wealth of the rich!

TERENCE (*Publius Terentius Afer*)

There is nothing more dangerous than to build a society with a large segment of people in that society who feel that they have no stake in it; who feel that they have nothing to lose. People who have stake in their society, protect that society, but when they don't have it, they unconsciously want to destroy it.

MARTIN LUTHER KING, JR.

We have to give our children, especially black boys, something to lose. Children make foolish choices when they have nothing to lose.

JAWANZA KUNJUFU

Hungry men have no respect for law, authority, or human life.

MARCUS GARVEY

I find it hard to deplore these percentages [of blacks in the military] because they represent blacks rushing through a door that some of us opened with great work and risk.

CARL T. ROWAN

This is our country. We don't have to slip around like peons or thieves in the middle of the night, asking someone for open sesame. Knock the damn door down!

HAROLD WASHINGTON

We don't hate nobody because of their color. We hate *oppression!*

BOBBY SEALE

White Americans today don't know what in the world to do because when they put us behind them, that's where they made their mistake. If they had put us in front, they wouldn't have let us look back. But they put us behind them, and we watched every move they made. . . .

FANNIE LOU HAMER

Racism systematically verifies itself
anytime the slave can only be free
by imitating his master.

JAMIL ABDULLAH AL-AMIN *(H. Rap Brown)*

It has been the fashion of [Euro-]
American writers to deny that the
Egyptians were Negroes and claim
that they are of the same race as
themselves. This has, I have no
doubt, been largely due to a wish to
deprive the Negro of the moral
support of Ancient Greatness and
to appropriate the same to the
white race.

FREDERICK DOUGLASS, *1887*

It is not so much a Negro History Week as it is History Week. We should emphasize not Negro History, but the Negro in history. What we need is not a history of selected races or nations, but the history of the world void of national bias, race hate and religious prejudice.

CARTER G. WOODSON, *1926*

. . . Historical facts are all pervasive and cut through the most rigid barriers of race and caste.

JOHN HOPE FRANKLIN, *1947*

History, as taught in our schools, has been a celebration of the white, male, Protestant Founding Fathers rather than the great mix of people in the American drama. . . . People who are in subordinated groups want history simply to do for them what history has already done for white males.

MARY FRANCES BERRY, *1991*

Education is the primary tool of emancipation and liberation for African-Americans in our fight for true equality in this country.

EARL G. GRAVES

If you can't count, they can cheat
you. If you can't read, they can beat
you.

TONI MORRISON

We have transformed few minds.
We have made no radical changes in
the economic servitude of the black
masses.

ADAM CLAYTON POWELL, JR.

When we were not paying enough
attention to the needs of the poor
and dysfunctional, they were
physically reproducing themselves.

LORRAINE HALE

The wretched of the earth do not decide to become extinct, they resolve, on the contrary, to multiply: life is their weapon against life, life is all that they have.

JAMES BALDWIN

The economic philosophy of black nationalism only means that our people need to be re-educated into the importance of controlling the economy of the community in which we live . . . which . . . means that we . . . won't have to constantly be involved in picketing and boycotting other people in other communities in order to get jobs.

MALCOLM X

I have the people behind me and the people are my strength.

HUEY P. NEWTON

The fear that had shackled us all across the years left us suddenly when we were in that church, together.

RALPH DAVID ABERNATHY

I know one thing we did right
Was the day we started to fight
Keep your eyes on the prize
Hold on. . . .

CIVIL RIGHTS MOVEMENT SONG

Too many of us are hung up on what we don't have, can't have, or won't ever have. We spend too much energy being down, when we could use that same energy—if not less of it—doing, or at least trying to do, some of the things we really want to do.

TERRY MCMILLAN

It . . . occurred to me that a system of oppression draws much of its strength from the acquiescence of its victims who have accepted the dominant image of themselves and are paralyzed by a sense of helplessness.

PAULI MURRAY

Strength abounds in Harlem. Three hundred years of oppression and it survives. This is the task in Harlem, to see strength where it exists, to expect it to be there. . . . Even anger may show strength. It can sustain a child and protect him until he is helped to find more suitable vehicles for his ability to love and to act.

MARGARET LAWRENCE

It is not enviable to be feared, but it is preferable to being lynched.

RALPH WILEY

Violence is as American as cherry
pie.

H. RAP BROWN *(Jamil Abdullah Al-Amin)*

And if sun comes
How shall we greet him?
Shall we not dread him,
Shall we not fear him
After so lengthy a
Session with shade?

GWENDOLYN BROOKS

Only the fool points at his origins
with his left hand.

AKAN PROVERB

Be not discouraged. There is a
future for you. . . . The resistance
encountered now predicates hope. . . .
Only as we rise . . . do we encounter
opposition.

FREDERICK DOUGLASS, *1892*

PRIDE

If you haven't got it, you can't show it. If you have got it, you can't hide it.

ZORA NEALE HURSTON

We wish to plead our own cause. Too long have others spoken for us. . . . Our vices and degradation are ever arrayed against us, but our virtues are passed by unnoticed.

JOHN RUSSWURM
SAMUEL CORNISH, *1827*

I will not leave South Africa, nor will I surrender. The struggle is my life. I will continue fighting for freedom until the end of my days.

NELSON MANDELA, *1961*

Power concedes nothing without a demand. It never did and it never will. Find out just what any people will quietly submit to and you have found out the exact measure of injustice and wrong that will be imposed upon them, and these will continue till they are resisted with either words or blows or with both. The limits of tyrants are prescribed by the endurance of those whom they oppress.

FREDERICK DOUGLASS, *1857*

The only protection against injustice in man is power—physical, financial and scientific.

MARCUS GARVEY

Let your motto be resistance!
resistance! RESISTANCE!
No oppressed people have ever
secured their liberty without
resistance.

HENRY HIGHLAND GARNET, *1843*

In Africa, there are no niggers; and
I will die before I become a nigger
for your entertainment.

VERNON REID

I have cherished the ideal of a democratic and free society in which all persons live together in harmony with equal opportunities. It is an ideal which I hope to live for and to see realized. But, if needs be, it is an ideal for which I am prepared to die.

NELSON MANDELA, *1964, 1990*

Brothers, we have done that which we purposed . . . we have striven to regain the precious heritage we received from our fathers. . . . I am resolved that it is better to die than be a white man's slave, and I will not complain if by dying I save you.

JOSEPH CINQUEZ, *1839*

Stop using the word "Negro." The word is a misnomer from every point of view. It does not represent a country or anything else. . . . I am an African-American. . . . I am not ashamed of my African descent. . . . After people have been freed, it is a cruel injustice to call them by the same name they bore as slaves.

MARY CHURCH TERRELL, *1949*

It's not what you call us, but what we answer to that matters.

DJUKA

I would fight for my liberty so long as my strength lasted, and if the time came for me to go, the Lord would let them take me.

HARRIET TUBMAN

There was only one thing I could do—hammer relentlessly, continually crying aloud, even if in a wilderness, and force open, by sheer muscle power, every closed door.

ADAM CLAYTON POWELL, JR.

What we see on the horizon is not the death of black politics but its growth and maturation.

EDDIE N. WILLIAMS

We understand that politics is
nothing but war without bloodshed;
and war is nothing but politics with
bloodshed.

FRED HAMPTON

A government which uses force
to maintain its rule teaches the
oppressed to use force to oppose it.

NELSON MANDELA

. . . **I**t doesn't mean that I advocate
violence, but at the same time I am
not against using violence in self-
defense. I don't even call it violence
when it's self-defense, I call it
intelligence.

MALCOLM X

Violence is black children going to
school for 12 years and receiving
6 years' worth of education.

JULIAN BOND

The truth about injustice always
sounds outrageous.

JAMES H. CONE

Truth knows no color; it appeals to
intelligence.

RALPH WILEY

Truth is that which serves the interests of a people. Two groups of people locked in combat cannot be expected to have the same truth.

ALBERT B. CLEAGE, JR.

. . . It is time for blacks to begin the shift from a wartime to a peacetime identity, from fighting for opportunity to the seizing of it.

SHELBY STEELE

. . . We are a Black Gold Mine. And the key that unlocks the door to these vast riches is the knowledge of who we are—I mean, who we *really* are.

TONY BROWN

There is a "sanctity" involved with bringing a child into this world; it is better than bombing one out of it.

JAMES BALDWIN

I have always been against the death penalty. . . . I believe it is a relic of barbarism and savagery and that it is inconsistent with decent morals and the teaching of Christian ethics.

KWAME NKRUMAH

. . . Violence always rebounds, always returns home.

LERONE BENNETT, JR.

The solution to poverty is not combating fertility. It's creating opportunities.

WALTER ALLEN

Every man has a right to his own opinion. Every race has a right to its own action; therefore let no man persuade you against your will, let no other race influence you against your own.

MARCUS GARVEY, *1923*

We ain't what we want to be; we ain't what we gonna be; but thank God, we ain't what we was.

AFRICAN-AMERICAN FOLK SAYING

CHALLENGE

We wanted something for
ourselves and for our
children, so we took a
chance with our lives.

UNITA BLACKWELL

Presumption should never make us neglect that which appears easy to us, nor despair make us lose courage at the sight of difficulties.

BENJAMIN BANNEKER, *1794*

Education remains the key to both economic and political empowerment.

BARBARA JORDAN, *1991*

The mere imparting of information is not education. Above all things, the effort must result in making a man think and do for himself.

CARTER G. WOODSON, *1933*

A child cannot be taught by someone who despises him.

JAMES BALDWIN

We must nurture our children with confidence. They can't make it if they are constantly told that they won't.

GEORGE CLEMENTS

No one rises to low expectations.

LES BROWN

The only justification for ever looking down on somebody is to pick them up.

JESSE L. JACKSON

. . . People who hurt other people have usually been hurt so badly themselves that all they know how to do is hurt back.

TERRY MCMILLAN

I never considered my race as a barrier to me. In fact, it's become an asset because it allows me to have a broader perspective.

JAMES G. KAISER

What you want to defeat is the idea that says your individuality doesn't count—that all you are is black. You want to say, "But I'm a person. Not a political entity."

JAMAICA KINCAID

Because I want every kid to be viewed as a person rather than as a member of a certain race does not mean that I'm not black enough. . . . Do they want me to be positive just for black kids and negative for everybody else?

MICHAEL JORDAN

The mind does not take its complexion from the skin. . . .

FREDERICK DOUGLASS, *1849*

Blackness is not a hairstyle. It is not a dashiki. Judge my blackness by the jobs that we have, by the money we are able to generate in the community. . . .

BERTHA KNOX GILKEY

Why pose and posture a self that is other than you, when I know your true name.

LEON FORREST

Dissension is healthy, even when it gets loud.

JENNIFER LAWSON

It ain't nothing to find no starting place in the world. You just start from where you find yourself.

AUGUST WILSON

It is critical that we take charge of our own destiny and stop waiting for some unknown mythical being to come along and wipe racism from the face of this earth.

DAVID C. WILSON

Can't nothin make your life work
if you ain't the architect.

TERRY MCMILLAN

The only protection against
genocide is to remain necessary.

JESSE L. JACKSON

A people who are truly strong
should be able to look soberly at
both their accomplishments and
their problems—past and present.

MICHAEL BLAKEY

Knowledge of one's identity, one's self, community, nation, religion and God, is the true meaning of resurrection, while ignorance of it signifies hell.

ELIJAH MUHAMMAD

It's better to be prepared for an opportunity and not have one than to have an opportunity and not be prepared.

WHITNEY YOUNG

I had to make my own living and my own opportunity. . . . Don't sit down and wait for the opportunities to come; you have to get up and make them.

MADAME C.J. WALKER, *1914*

Opportunity follows struggle. It follows effort. It follows hard work. It doesn't come before.

SHELBY STEELE, *1991*

When you are looking for obstacles, you can't find opportunities.

J.C. BELL

The individual who can do something that the world wants done will, in the end, make his way regardless of his race.

BOOKER T. WASHINGTON, *1901*

It would be against all nature for all the Negroes to be either at the bottom, top, or in between. . . . We will go where the internal drive carries us like everybody else. It is up to the individual.

ZORA NEALE HURSTON, *1942*

Our elevation must be the result of self-efforts, and work of our own hands. No other human power can accomplish it. If we but determine it shall be so, it will be so.

MARTIN R. DELANY, *1852*

I have discovered in life that there are ways of getting almost anywhere you want to go, if you really want to go.

LANGSTON HUGHES

A person without faith has no future.

MICHAEL J. CHEATHAM

... The tragedy in life doesn't lie in not reaching your goal. The tragedy lies in having no goal to reach. It isn't a calamity to die with dreams unfulfilled, but it is certainly a calamity not to dream. It is not a disaster to be unable to capture your ideal, but it is a disaster to have no ideal to capture.

BENJAMIN E. MAYS

If you run, you might lose. If you don't run, you're guaranteed to lose.

JESSE L. JACKSON

Fortune favors the bold.

TERENCE *(Publius Terentius Afer)*

How can a man live out the length of his fiery days without a vision-prize?

LEON FORREST

If you don't dream, you might as well be dead.

GEORGE FOREMAN

When life knocks you down, try to fall on your back because if you can look up, you can get up.

LES BROWN

In every crisis there is a message. Crises are nature's way of forcing change—breaking down old structures, shaking loose negative habits so that something new and better can take their place.

SUSAN L. TAYLOR

I believe . . . that living on the edge, living in and through your fear, is the summit of life, and that people who refuse to take that dare condemn themselves to a life of living death.

JOHN H. JOHNSON

I don't know the key to success, but the key to failure is trying to please everybody.

BILL COSBY

The thing that makes you exceptional, if you are at all, is inevitably that which must also make you lonely.

LORRAINE HANSBERRY

Where is the power? Not on the outside, but within. . . . Thoughts are things. You are the thinker that thinks the thought, that makes the thing. If you don't like it, then change your thoughts. Make it what you want it to be.

JOHNNIE COLEMON

You have to know that your real home is within.

QUINCY JONES

. . . **O**ut of the heart are the issues of life and no external force, however great and overwhelming, can at long last destroy a people if it does not first win the victory of the spirit against them.

HOWARD THURMAN

If I didn't define myself for myself, I would be crunched into other people's fantasies for me and eaten alive.

AUDRE LORDE

Whatever we believe about ourselves and our ability comes true for us.

SUSAN L. TAYLOR

INDEX

NAME

ACKNOWLEDGMENTS

Excerpt from "forgiving my father" by Lucille Clifton reprinted by permission of Curtis Brown, Ltd. © 1980 by The University of Massachusetts Press.

Excerpt from the poem "I Am A Black Woman" by Mari Evans on page 14 reprinted by permission of the author.

By the same author

Famous Black Quotations
and some not so famous

Also, look for
Famous Black Quotations®
bookmarks and note cards.

Typeset in Palatino by **murray/tgm,**
Chicago.

✂

Please send me _____ copies of FAMOUS BLACK QUOTATIONS *on women, love and other topics* at $5.95.

Please send me _____ copies of FAMOUS BLACK QUOTATIONS *and some not so famous* at $3.99.

☐ Please send me information on other FAMOUS BLACK QUOTATIONS products.

your name _____ phone: area code/number _____

shipping address _____

city _____ state _____ zip _____

Add $1.50 shipping plus 50¢ for each additional item. Total enclosed $ _____

Include payment with order. Make checks or money orders payable to SABAYT PUBLICATIONS.

Sabayt Publications
P.O. Box 64898
Chicago, Illinois 60664-0898
312/667-2227

(PLEASE ALLOW 3–4 WEEKS FOR DELIVERY.)